P9-AQX-322

Excalibur

FRANKLIN PIERCE
COLLEGE LIBRARY
RINDGE, N.H. 03461

TALES OF KING ARTHUR

Excalibur

written and illustrated by
HUDSON TALBOTT

Books of Wonder   Morrow Junior Books   New York

Watercolors were used for the full-color illustrations.
The text type is 15-point Goudy Old Style.

Copyright © 1996 by Hudson Talbott
Afterword copyright © 1996 by Peter Glassman

All rights reserved. No part of this book may be reproduced or utilized in any form or by
any means, electronic or mechanical, including photocopying, recording, or by any information storage
and retrieval system, without permission in writing from the Publisher. Inquiries should be addressed to
William Morrow and Company, Inc., 1350 Avenue of the Americas, New York, NY 10019, or
Books of Wonder, 132 Seventh Avenue at Eighteenth Street, New York, NY 10011.
Printed in Singapore at Tien Wah Press.
1 3 5 7 9 10 8 6 4 2

Library of Congress Cataloging-in-Publication Data
Talbott, Hudson.
Excalibur/by Hudson Talbott.
p. cm.—(Books of wonder)
Summary: The young King Arthur asks for and receives the
noble sword Excalibur from the Lady of the Lake and promises
to be deserving of it through acts of valor.
ISBN 0-688-13380-0 (trade)—ISBN 0-688-13381-9 (library)
1. Arthurian romances—Adaptations.   [1. Arthur, King—Legends.
2. Knights and knighthood—Folklore.   3. Folklore—England.]
I. Title.   II. Series.
PZ8.1.T132Ex 1996   398.2'094202—dc20   [E]   95-35388   CIP AC

Books of Wonder is a registered trademark of Ozma, Inc.

CURR
PZ
7
.T153
EXC
1996

For the Mother Spirit,
and my mom in particular

ritain was still a young nation when a Welsh country
lad named Arthur became its high king, or Pendragon.
He had proven his birthright by pulling the Pendragon sword
out of a stone when no one else could.

But Arthur also wanted to prove himself worthy of lead-
ing his countrymen and used the sword to rally them against
their common foe, the Saxons. By the time they had driven the
invaders from their shores, the Britons were united behind their
brave new leader, and young Arthur's fame soon spread
throughout the world.

The finest knights had come forth to join Arthur in his campaign against the Saxons, and they rejoiced in their victory together. But with peace returning, each knight soon felt the urge to find his own path again, and one by one they excused themselves from Arthur's company.

"I hear there's a giant causing trouble down in Cornwall," called Sir Ulfius as he waved farewell.

"A dragon was seen in Loch Ness again," said Sir Sagrimore. "*I'll* take care of it this time."

"I'll ride along with you to Glastonbury," said Sir Lionel. "There's a damsel held in a tower by the local witch."

By the time Arthur reached his castle at Caerleon he was left with only his adviser, Merlin, and a handful of older knights who amused themselves with boasts of their own youthful adventures.

Day after day, Arthur heard tales of others' glory, and soon his pride in his own achievements gave way to envy.

"I need a quest!" he complained to Merlin. "A knight has more fun than a king."

"Each of us has a unique destiny, sire," said Merlin. "There's much to be gained by understanding your role in life and much to be lost by ignoring it."

Their attention was suddenly drawn to young Sir Griflet, who was returning, badly wounded, from his first quest. He had lost a joust with a knight who blocked a bridge and dared any of Arthur's men to cross it.

That knight is challenging *me*, of course, thought Arthur.

"You are not free to endanger yourself the way your knights do, Your Majesty," said Merlin abruptly.

"Merlin!" boomed Arthur. "Have I no privacy? Do you read all my thoughts?"

"Just enough to worry me, sire," replied the wizard. "That hostile knight is King Pellinore, one of the fiercest warriors in all of Britain. He is still angry for not being chosen high king himself and would certainly kill you now. But if you leave him alone, he will soon come around and someday make a fine ally."

Arthur nodded blandly, but early the next morning he quietly saddled his horse and slipped out of the palace alone.

After riding for hours through field and forest Arthur dismounted at a spring, where he lay down to rest. But he was soon startled awake by another thirsty visitor. Drinking from the fountain was the legendary creature known as the Questing Beast.

Arthur stood transfixed until someone in the forest called to him: "I say there, lad! Did an odd-looking beast pass your way?"

"Why, yes! It's right here!" Arthur called back. But when he turned around, the beast was gone.

The stranger quickly made his way toward Arthur.

"Perhaps I should take on your quest," Arthur said. "After all, you're on foot, and I have a—"

"There's a good lad. Help me up!" said the knight, climbing onto Arthur's horse.

"Excuse me, but that's *my* horse!"

"And it's *my quest*!" retorted the knight as he rode away. "If you wish to make it yours, you may find me tomorrow at the old Roman bridge."

"What? Come back here!" yelled Arthur, running after him.

"Let him go," murmured a voice from the woods. "You have more important things to do. Pellinore does not."

"Pellinore?" said Arthur, looking around. "That rogue stole my horse!"

"You're fortunate that's all he took," said Merlin, stepping from the shadows. "A king's duty is to his people, not to his pride."

But Merlin had barely spoken the words when Arthur turned sharply and stormed away.

The next morning Arthur found his way to the bridge and pounded loudly on his shield, the signal for jousting. The curtains of the nearby tent slowly parted, and there stood the ominous figure of King Pellinore.

"Oh, it's *you*, lad!" he said, smirking. "Well, I shall let you go this time, because of the foolishness of your youth. But I must have your shield as the price for disturbing my slumber."

"Sir Knight, you have insulted me," countered Arthur fiercely. "Make ready for combat."

"As you wish, boy. But your coat of arms shall enter my collection in any case," said the nobleman, gesturing toward a tree hung with battered shields.

Pellinore mounted his horse, trotted a short distance, and then wheeled around to face Arthur. The two kings leveled their spears, readied their shields, and then spurred their chargers into a thunderous gallop toward each other.

Arthur's spear shattered on impact, but Pellinore's blow sent Arthur flying. The younger king barely escaped the crush of his own horse as both tumbled to the ground.

Pellinore turned and dismounted. "I'll take no advantage over you, lad," he said with a grin. "I'll beat you fairly on the ground."

The two warriors drew their swords and lunged at each other. Arthur's speed and agility were easily matched by the sheer power of the mighty Pellinore. For hours they slashed and jabbed at each other, till both were staggering and drenched in blood.

Finally, sensing his moment, Pellinore brought his sword down with all his remaining strength. Arthur raised his sword instinctively, but this time it broke under Pellinore's devastating blow. The legendary Pendragon sword fell to the ground in pieces, leaving Arthur defenseless.

"Now, sire, yield to me or ye shall die," said Pellinore, gasping for breath. He pulled out his dagger and pressed it against Arthur's throat.

"As for death, I welcome it, if it is my time," said Arthur. "I yield only to God, sire."

"Then so be it," said Pellinore, pressing forward.

Suddenly the dagger fell away from Arthur's throat. He looked up to see the gigantic knight falling backward to lie motionless. Merlin stepped out of the bushes.

"What have you done?" moaned Arthur. "You've killed this great knight with your tricks when I couldn't beat him fairly! Let me die! Let me die!"

"He's only asleep," said Merlin. "I had to do *something*. But *you* will die if we do not tend your wounds immediately!"

But Arthur was already unconscious. Merlin brought him to the forest dwelling of a hermit who knew the healing arts. After treating the king's wounds, the two old men sat down to pray and wait.

Fever drove Arthur into the nightmarish realm between life and death. The old men tended his wounds, but Arthur alone had to face the fiery visions burning his mind. For three days and nights he writhed in agony.

Finally Arthur's fever broke, and his strength slowly returned. But he seemed distant and sad.

After days of riding in silence, Merlin asked Arthur why he remained so troubled. The youth was slow to respond.

"Because I've let you down," he said at last. "I wanted you to be proud of me, but who am I? A defeated king…a swordless knight…a nothing."

"Arthur," said Merlin gently. "Just as there is more to a knight than his sword, there is far more to a king than his crown. Sooner or later we must all face a defeat. Greatness lives in one who knows how to learn from victory *or* defeat and goes on to carry out his duty."

Arthur smiled at Merlin for the first time in days. "That is what matters to me now," he said. "But I still need a sword in order to carry out *my* duty."

"That is why we've come to this land," said Merlin. "There is a great sword not far from here, crafted by the fairy folk."

Arthur quietly gazed at the landscape before them. Its unearthly beauty mystified him until he slowly realized that they had somehow crossed into the enchanted realm.

"This is Avalon," said Merlin, "the domain of the Lady of the Lake. Deep within these waters rests her greatest possession: the noble sword Excalibur. She has long held it in safekeeping for the one who is meant to use it."

As the mists shifted on the lake, a figure could be seen gliding over the surface toward them. "Greetings, Sir King," called the Lady of the Lake softly. Arthur waded knee deep into the water and bowed.

"My lady, I've come to ask your help. I have broken my sword and cannot fulfill my duty without one. I would that the noble sword Excalibur were mine."

"Do you deserve it?" she asked calmly.

"I cannot yet say, my lady, for I have only just opened my eyes," said Arthur. "But upon my honor as king, I shall dedicate my life to proving that I do."

The Lady of the Lake gazed down at Arthur. "Then so it shall be," she said, and presented him with the sword's scabbard. "May Excalibur be of service to you that you may be of service to the world." She pointed to the center of the lake, where a golden blade rose above the water. "Return Excalibur to the lake when your life's work is done."

A small boat appeared, sailing smoothly toward the shore. Arthur and Merlin stepped into it.

Arthur took the sword and slid it into the scabbard. "Excalibur…," he whispered. "May I be worthy of you."

As they drifted back to shore, Merlin quietly observed the reverence with which Arthur handled Excalibur. The old man realized that somewhere over the waters of Avalon, the innocent lad from Wales had disappeared forever. In his place now sat an earnest young man, ready to serve his people with grace and dignity.

"Which do you prefer, the sword or the scabbard?" asked Merlin.

"The sword, of course!" said Arthur. "It's magnificent."

"The scabbard would be the wiser choice," Merlin advised him. "The sword will, indeed, slay any opponent, but the scabbard will protect you. As long as you wear it, you will never lose a drop of blood, no matter how wounded you are."

"Then I shall never be without it," said Arthur. This comforted the old man, for he knew his time of watching over Arthur was nearing its end.

"Let's go home, Your Majesty," said Merlin.

When Arthur and Merlin returned to Caerleon, they were surprised by the sight of the king's men waiting to welcome them home. For all the knights' adventures, there was never a happier moment for any in that noble company than the morning King Arthur returned with Excalibur.

As Arthur raised the great sword, he noticed a dark figure coming through the cheering assembly. The men grew silent and stepped back when they saw that Pellinore was in their midst.

"Your Majesty, I have come to ask forgiveness," said Pellinore. "I did not know who you were, but now I do. Only a Pendragon could have such valor. I wish to join your company so that I too may champion your cause."

Arthur dismounted and walked toward the kneeling king, then touched his shoulders with the point of Excalibur and said: "Rise, Sir Pellinore, and find your place among our fellow-ship. May your courage always be guided by your wisdom."

AFTERWORD

The legends of King Arthur and the Knights of the Round Table have delighted readers of all ages for hundreds of years. And the story of how Arthur acquired his magical sword, Excalibur, is among the most popular of these tales.

Stories about King Arthur date back over a thousand years, and books about his and his knights' adventures can be found as far back as the fifteenth century. In fact, King Arthur was the subject of one of the first books ever printed in England—Sir Thomas Malory's *Morte Darthur*. Produced in 1485 by the great English printer William Caxton, this book is considered by many to be the definitive work about Arthur and the Round Table.

But like all great myths and legends, the tales of King Arthur were told and retold by many different people for hundreds of years before they were ever put down in the pages of a book. No one person can be credited with the many stories of the Round Table, in which each generation finds new meaning and the inspiration to create its own versions of these legends.

The story of Excalibur is particularly enduring, because it tells of how Arthur comes of age. In "The Sword in the Stone," Arthur learns to accept that fate has decreed a role of fame and leadership for him, one that changes his young life irrevocably. But it is in "Excalibur" that he grows up and comes to terms with the immense responsibilities of being king.

Hudson Talbott has crafted this legend into a moving tale in which Arthur achieves mastery over his own pride and impulsiveness through defeat at King Pellinore's hands. It is easy to believe that this noble young man will go on to found the legendary Round Table and its order of knights devoted to using their might to help the less fortunate.

—*Peter Glassman*

FRANKLIN PIERCE COLLEGE LIBRARY

00098170